NERVES
BRAIN & SENSES

by
STEVE PARKER
Consultant
DR KRISTINA ROUTH

HOW TO USE THIS BOOK

This book is your guide to yourself – an atlas of the human body. Follow the main text to get an informative overview of a particular area of the body, or use the boxes to jump to a specific area of interest. Finally, there are even experiments for you to try yourself!

Body Locator

The highlighted areas on the body locator tell you immediately which areas of the body you are learning about. This will help you to understand your body's geography.

Instant Facts

This box gives you snappy facts that summarise the topic in just a few sentences. Find out how how fast nerve signals travel, how many smells we can detect and much more.

Healthwatch

Go here to read about illness and disease related to the relevant area of the body. For example, find out about what can happen if the brain suffers a heavy blow, and what we can do to protect ourselves.

INSTANT FACT

Short-term memories last a few seconds or minutes. They are information we know we won't need to keep for long, like a little-used phone number before we call it.

Medium-term memories last a few hours or days, like what we ate during meals yesterday.

Long-term memories last many years, even a lifetime.

The life of any memory depends on how often it is 'refreshed' by thinking about it and recalling it regularly.

HEALTHWATCH
Everyone is forgetful now and then. Often there are reasons, such as too much to do in too short a time. This leads to mental stress, when the brain is so busy with jumbled thoughts that it cannot cope with the information.

14

BRAIN *Learning & Memory*

Can you remember your name? Your ho address and phone number? The answer questions will probably be yes. What ab number of windows in your home? That might be more di

FINDING MEMORIES You might be able to answer the question abou windows by using your memory in another way. In your imagination, go into a room in your house. You can see the windows in your 'mind's eye'. Count their number. Do this for each room, add up all the windows, and you have the answer. This shows how we remember not only names, faces, facts and places, and lessons we learn at school. We can recall scene feelings, smells, sounds and countless other memories.

SHORT & LONG No one really knows where this information is stored. A computer has a hard disc and where it stores most of its information. But there is no single place like a 'hard disc' in the brain. Many brain parts work together to learn, make memories and then recall them. They include the outer layer of the cortex, and under it the thalamus, amygdala and hippocampus. A memory is probably a particular set of connections or pathways between the billions of nerve cells. Learning a new fact involves making a new set of connections.

OUR MEMORY FOR FACES IS ESPECIALLY AMAZING. Some people can tell apart more th faces from photographs, after seeing each one for just two seconds.

Try it Yourself

Activity boxes with exercises that you can try yourself. No special equipment required – just your own body!

In Focus

This panel takes a really close look at one aspect of the human body, using stunningly detailed macro-imagery and stills taken from an anatomically correct digital model of human anatomy.

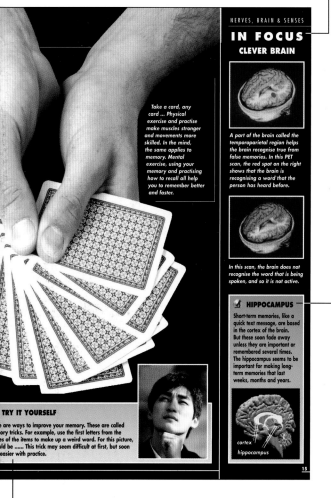

Take a card, any card ... Physical exercise and practise make muscles stronger and movements more skilled. In the mind, the same applies to memory. Mental exercise, using your memory and practising how to recall all help you to remember better and faster.

NERVES, BRAIN & SENSES

IN FOCUS
CLEVER BRAIN

A part of the brain called the temporoparietal region helps the brain recognise true from false memories. In this PET scan, the red spot on the right shows that the brain is recognising a word that the person has heard before.

In this scan, the brain does not recognise the word that is being spoken, and so it is not active.

HIPPOCAMPUS

Short-term memories, like a quick text message, are based in the cortex of the brain. But these soon fade away unless they are important or remembered several times. The hippocampus seems to be important for making long-term memories that last weeks, months and years.

cortex
hippocampus

15

TRY IT YOURSELF
...e are ways to improve your memory. These are called
...ory tricks. For example, use the first letters from the
...es of the items to make up a weird word. For this picture,
...ld be ...... This trick may seem difficult at first, but soon
...easier with practice.

Diagrams

Go to this box for scientific diagrams complete with annotations that tell you exactly what you are looking at.

INTRODUCTION

How many thoughts have you had today? How often have you used your memory since you woke up? Think hard, and try to remember ... But it's probably impossible. Thinking and remembering are such important parts of life, we do them all the time – without noticing!

THE PUZZLE OF THE BRAIN Thoughts and memories happen in the brain. The workings of the brain are among the greatest challenges for scientists. Every year we learn more about the dozens of different parts inside the brain, and how they send nerve signals to and fro, millions of times every second. These nerve signals are the way we think, remember, decide, carry out actions and movements, have feelings and emotions, and understand. But the brain is so complicated that it seems the more we know, the more there is to find out.

THE BODY'S 'INTERNET' Part of the challenge is that the brain does not work by itself. It is linked to all parts of the body and communicates with them by an amazing network of branching, wire-like parts called nerves. These carry vast amounts of information to and from the brain, and all around the body, at incredible speed. The nerve system is like the global Internet, but all packed into one human shape.

SENSING THE SURROUNDINGS Like a supercomputer, the brain can do little without information coming into it. This information comes from the body's senses. It's often said that there are five senses: sight, hearing, smell, taste and touch. However, the body's sensory system, like the brain and nerves, is much more complex than it seems, as this book will show.

NERVES, BRAIN AND SPINAL CORD COMBINE TO MAKE UP YOUR NERVOUS SYSTEM. The billions of nerves in your nervous system control everything you do both consciously and unconsciously, from breathing to sensing pain.

THE HUMAN BRAIN IS THE MOST POWERFUL COMPUTER IN THE WORLD. Although it weighs just over a kilogram, it controls all of our thoughts and actions, and enables us to achieve great practical and creative feats.

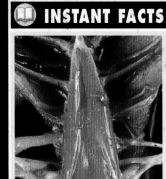
NERVES *THE NERVOUS SYSTEM*

People who are 'nervous' are jumpy and edgy, slightly worried and tense. But in one way, everyone is nervous all the time. The body's nerves are always working, carrying astonishing amounts of information in the form of tiny electrical pulses called nerve signals.

If all the body's nerves were joined end to end **they would stretch about 100 km.**

The thickest main nerve is the **sciatic nerve in the hip and thigh**, which is as wide as your thumb.

The longest nerve is the tibial nerve, which runs from above the knee almost down to the ankle.

A place where several nerves come together and branch again in **a small network is called a plexus.**

THREE PARTS IN ONE

The nervous system is really three systems combined into one. The largest part of the entire nerve network is the brain. The base of the brain joins to the body's main nerve, the spinal cord, which runs down the inside of the neck and back. The brain and spinal cord together are called the central nervous system. This is because they are central to the way the system works, in the way that a central computer controls many devices and machines attached to it.

EVERY SECOND THE BRAIN TAKES IN HUGE AMOUNTS OF INFORMATION from the senses and sends out millions of signals to control the body's hundreds of muscles. This is why we sometimes have to concentrate really hard to complete difficult tasks, such as jet skiing or other sports.

IN FOCUS
HEAD & FACE

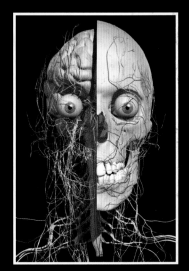

An intricate network of small nerves links the brain to the muscles and skin of the head and face. These are among the body's most touch-sensitive parts with precise muscle control.

SUPPORT SYSTEMS The second part of the nerve network is known as the peripheral nervous system. It is made up of all the nerves that branch from the brain and spinal cord out to various parts of the head and body. The third part of the nerve network is called the autonomic nerve system. It is made up of areas inside the brain and spinal cord, and other nerves that run down the back, on either side of the spinal cord, and into body parts like the lungs, guts and heart. The autonomic nerve system controls processes that happen automatically, without us thinking about them. These include digesting food and making the heart beat.

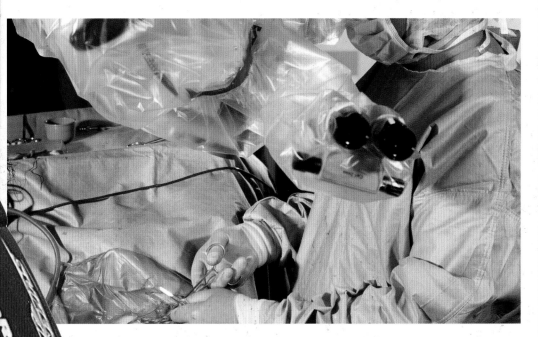

NERVES ARE SOME OF THE BODY'S MOST DELICATE, EASILY-HARMED PARTS. *Neurosurgeons are doctors who specialize in operations on the brain and nerves, dealing with single nerve fibres that are thinner than human hairs.*

🖐 TRY IT YOURSELF

Have you felt the tingling sensation of 'pins and needles', after sitting awkwardly, or applying pressure on part of the body? This feeling warns that a nerve is being squashed, or the blood vessels bringing blood to it are being squeezed. Next time you get this feeling, move, stretch, exercise and rub the part as soon as possible to feel better.

⚡ TWO OUT OF THREE

The central nervous system is the brain's main control centre. The peripheral nervous system carries nerve impulses between the central nervous system and other parts of our body.

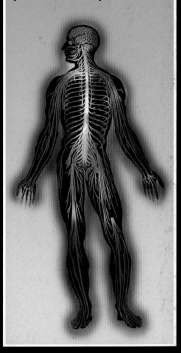

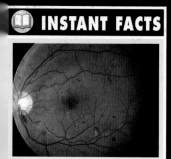
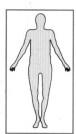

A single nerve signal lasts for 1/700th of a second.

Most nerve fibres can **carry up to 300 nerve signals per second.**

The fastest nerve signals travel at more than **200 metres per second,** so they can go from toe to brain in less than 1/100th of a second.

The slowest signals travel at **less than one metre per second.**

👁 **HEALTHWATCH**

Once a nerve is damaged or injured, it can take months or years to heal – if it ever does. It may not be able to carry signals to make muscles move, which is known as paralysis. Also, it may be unable to carry signals from the skin to the brain, so there is loss of feeling or numbness. Preventing nerve damage is one of many reasons to wear proper body protection like shoulder pads, elbow and knee guards, gloves and footwear, especially for risky activities and extreme sports.

NERVES *ALL ABOUT OUR NERVES*

Most parts of the body are repaired and replaced as they gradually wear away. The skin renews itself every month, and the inside of the stomach is replaced every three days. But nerves are different. They are so complicated that they rarely get repaired or renewed.

NERVE CELLS Inside every nerve, there are thousands of tiny thread-like fibres of microscopic nerve cells. The whole nervous system contains hundreds of billions of these complicated little cells. They carry tiny electrical signals, just like the wires inside a computer.

BECAUSE NERVES SNAKE BETWEEN ALL BODY PARTS, they need to be strong and flexible. They get bent when we move, squeezed by bulging muscles, and squashed when we sit and lie down.

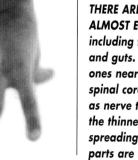

THERE ARE NERVES TO ALMOST EVERY BODY PART, including the heart, lungs and guts. The thickest ones near the brain and spinal cord are known as nerve trunks, while the thinnest ones spreading into body parts are terminal fibres.

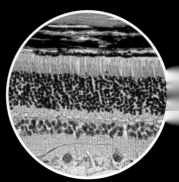

The ends of a nerve fibre are separated from other nerve cells by slight gaps called synapses. Electrical nerve signals 'jump' across these gaps in the form of natural body chemicals called neurotransmitters.

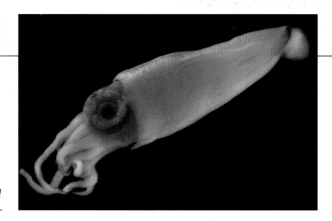

THE NERVE FIBRES IN THE HUMAN BODY are less than 1/1000th of one millimetre wide. In a squid, they are thicker than human hairs. Studying squid nerves has helped greatly to understand our own nervous system!

COMING & GOING On its own, a single nerve cell is not special. It simply passes on signals to other nerve cells. Linked together, however, these cells create something quite amazing. Each nerve cell receives signals from thousands of other cells, and passes on signals to thousands more. The numbers of different pathways for signals through the whole system, with billions of nerve cells, is almost endless. And every day, as we make decisions, imagine new thoughts, carry out actions and form memories, the pathways change.

TRY IT YOURSELF

When you hurt your toe or finger, you probably feel the touch on it first, within a split second. Then just afterwards, the pain starts. This usually happens because the signals about touch on the skin travel faster along nerves to the brain, than the signals about pain.

Each nerve cell has many spider-like 'wires' called dendrites. These receive nerve signals and lead to a main cell body. The very long fibre or axon is like a wire. It carries the signals along and passes them to other nerve cells, at junctions called synapses.

FASCICLES

The nerve's strong outer covering, the epineurium, contains bundles of nerve fibres, each fibre being too thin to see. The bundles, called fascicles, are surrounded by 'padding' to cushion the fibres as they bend and twist with body movements. Each fascicle encloses up to 200 nerve fibres.

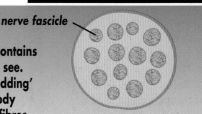

nerve fascicle

The average adult human **brain weighs 1,400 grams**.

It has more than **100 billion nerve cells**.

In normal health, there is **no link between brain size and intelligence** or cleverness.

Women have slightly larger brains in proportion to their body size, compared to men.

A new baby's brain is ⅓ of its adult size.

◉ HEALTHWATCH

Most people get occasional headaches. However, a person who develops a severe headache together with a stiff neck, aversion to bright lights and perhaps a skin rash, may have the serious infection of meningitis. This is swelling and pain in the meninges, which are wrap-around layers covering the brain. Meningitis needs medical attention without delay.

BRAIN *DRIVING FORCE*

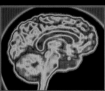

The brain looks like a lump of pinky-grey jelly. Despite its appearance, however, the brain is the place where we carry out mental processes, like thinking, remembering, feeling sensations and controlling our muscles. Surprisingly, however, the brain has no senses or muscles of its own.

AUTO-CONTROL The large, rounded, wrinkled part on top of the brain is called the cerebrum. One of the most important parts that lie underneath is the brain stem, which lies between the cerebrum and the spinal cord. The main job of the brain stem is to control automatic body processes. These include controlling the heartbeat, digesting food in the guts, overseeing our breathing, and keeping the body at a constant warm temperature.

cerebrum

cerebellum

thalamus

brain stem

spinal cord

🔧 BRAIN PARTS

This computer-generated graphic of a human brain shows the major parts, surrounded by the protective skull. The cerebrum is the area that controls most of our actions.

MAKING MOVEMENTS The lower rearmost part of the brain consists of another rounded, wrinkled part called the cerebellum. This makes up about one-tenth of the brain's total size, and controls the movement of our muscles. Nerve signals are sent down from the cerebrum to the cerebellum. Here the details of which muscles should tighten, and by how much, and for how long are worked out. This information helps the muscles work together as a team to make our movements smooth and precise.

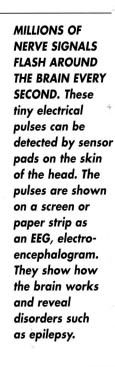

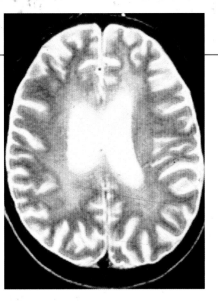

MRI (Magnetic Resonance Imaging) scans (above) show the details of the brain's inner structure, including its many blood vessels. These scans help to find problems such as lack of blood flow to part of the brain, which can cause the disorder known as a stroke.

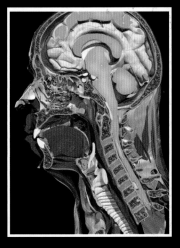

In the middle of the brain is a system of flattened hollow chambers called cerebral ventricles. They contain the same liquid that bathes the outside of the brain, known as cerebrospinal fluid.

MILLIONS OF NERVE SIGNALS FLASH AROUND THE BRAIN EVERY SECOND. These tiny electrical pulses can be detected by sensor pads on the skin of the head. The pulses are shown on a screen or paper strip as an EEG, electro-encephalogram. They show how the brain works and reveal disorders such as epilepsy.

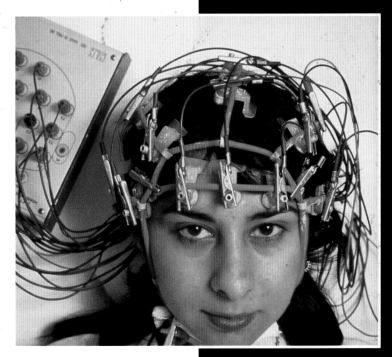

🖐 TRY IT YOURSELF

Gently tap the top of your head. It makes a dull thud. This is because underneath the skull, the brain is surrounded by a thin layer of liquid called cerebrospinal fluid. As the head twists and moves rapidly, or gets knocked, the fluid makes a moving cushion to protect the brain from damage.

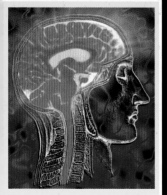

The outer layer or cortex of the brain, **spread out flat, would cover the area of a pillowcase**.

It contains **more than 50 billion nerve cells**.

Each of these nerve cells can have **connections with up to a quarter of a million other nerve cells**.

These **nerve cells give the cortex a greyish colour**, which is why the brain is sometimes called 'grey matter'.

HEALTHWATCH

The brain is well protected by the skull, and during risky activities it should also be guarded by a hard-hat, helmet or similar headgear. But sometimes a blow on the head shakes it so much the person becomes unconscious – concussed or 'knocked out'. If this happens, no matter how brief, medical attention is needed to prevent later problems.

BRAIN *Centres & Control*

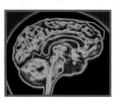

The mission control room at a space centre is full of people, screens and computers. Some plan the rocket's route, some receive information from the equipment on board, while others look after the fuel and engines. The brain inside your head works just like a complicated mission control room.

THE BODY'S MISSION CONTROL Over three-quarters of the brain is made up of the cerebrum. Its outer layer is called the cerebral cortex. This part of the brain acts as the body's 'mission control room'. The cerebral cortex is the main place where thinking happens, and where information is received from the senses, and sent out to the muscles. Like a control room, the cerebral cortex is highly organised. Different parts of the cortex, called centres, each deal with different jobs.

THE TWO SIDES OF THE BRAIN LOOK SIMILAR. But in most people they have slightly different roles. The left side takes the lead for step-by-step thoughts, reasoning, dealing with numbers and facts. The right side is more active in awareness of shapes, colours, musical sounds and artistic skills.

THE CEREBRUM HAS A VERY DEEP GROOVE ALONG THE MIDDLE FROM FRONT TO BACK, dividing it into two cerebral hemispheres. More deep grooves divide each hemisphere into five main sections or lobes.

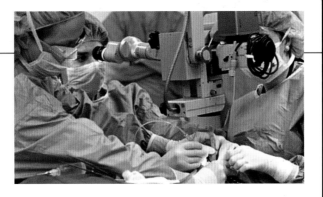

The brain has no sense of touch or pain. During surgery, it cannot feel the surgeon's cutting scalpels or laser beams. However, the brain coverings, or meninges, are very sensitive.

CENTRES FOR SENSES The lower part of the cortex is called the visual centre because it helps to control the sense of sight. Nerve signals arrive here from the eyes, and are processed and compared with information about scenes and objects already stored in the memory. The body's auditory (hearing) centre can be found on the sides of the brain. There is also a centre for taste (gustatory centre), and a touch centre, which runs in a strip from side to side, arching over the top of the brain.

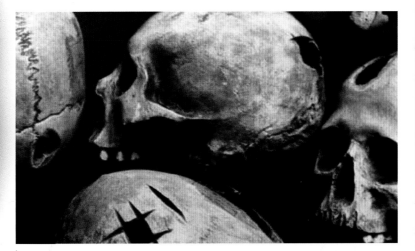

Archaeologists have found the skulls of people with holes drilled through them. Experts think these holes were made in an attempt to cure terrible headaches or release 'demons'. Remarkably, archaeologists can tell patients often survived this procedure, as lots of skulls with healed bone have been unearthed.

NERVES, BRAIN & SENSE

IN FOCUS
BRAIN HEMISPHERES

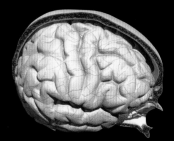

The upper front of each cerebral hemisphere is known as the frontal lobe. The frontal cortex covering it is important in what we call 'personality', and in the awareness of the body's position in its surroundings, so we don't bump into things!

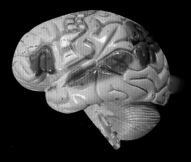

This coloured 'map' of the cortex shows the various centres for planning movements (very pale yellow) and making them (orange), touch on the skin (pale blue-grey), speech (blue), hearing (red) and vision at the brain's lower rear (dark yellow).

🦅 TRY IT YOURSELF

Can you write your name with your 'other' hand? Have a go. The first few tries will probably be terrible. Try 40 or 50 times, with short rests between. Compare the 50th attempt with the first. The motor centre in your brain has learned to control your hand and arm muscles to make a new pattern of movements.

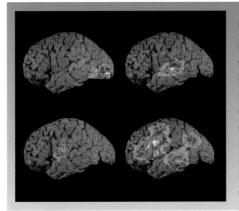

🔬 BUSY BRAIN

PET (positron emission tomography) scans show the brain's energy use and which regions are 'busiest'. This series of PET images shows the left side of the brain in a person who is staring (upper left), listening (upper right), speaking (lower left) and thinking about talking and moving (lower right).

Short-term memories last a few seconds or minutes. They are information we know we won't need to keep for long, like a little-used phone number before we call it.

Medium-term memories last a few hours or days, like what we ate during meals yesterday.

Long-term memories last many years, even a lifetime.

The life of any memory depends on how often it is 'refreshed' by thinking about it and recalling it regularly.

BRAIN *Learning & Memory*

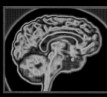

Can you remember your name? Your home address and phone number? The answer to these questions will probably be yes. What about the number of windows in your home? That might be more difficult.

FINDING MEMORIES You might be able to answer the question about windows by using your memory in another way. In your imagination, go into a room in your house. You can see the windows in your 'mind's eye'. Count their number. Do this for each room, add up all the windows, and you have the answer. This shows how we remember not only names, faces, facts and places, and lessons we learn at school. We can recall scenes, feelings, smells, sounds and countless other memories.

SHORT *&* LONG No one really knows where this information is stored. A computer has a hard disc where it stores most of its information. But there is no single place like a 'hard disc' in the brain. Many brain parts work together to learn, make memories and then recall them. They include the outer layer of the cortex, and under it the thalamus, amygdala and hippocampus. A memory is probably a particular set of connections or pathways between the billions of nerve cells. Learning a new fact involves making a new set of connections.

OUR MEMORY FOR FACES IS ESPECIALLY AMAZING. Some people can identify more than 100 faces from photographs, after seeing each one for just two seconds.

IN FOCUS
CLEVER BRAIN

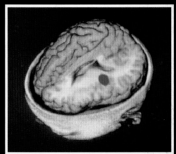

A part of the brain called the temporoparietal region helps the brain recognise true from false memories. In this PET scan, the red spot on the right shows that the brain is recognising a word that the person has heard before.

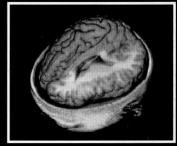

In this scan, the brain does not recognise the word that is being spoken, and so it is not active.

HIPPOCAMPUS

Short-term memories, like a quick text message, are based in the cortex of the brain. But these soon fade away unless they are important or remembered several times. The hippocampus seems to be important for making long-term memories that last weeks, months and years.

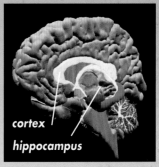

cortex

hippocampus

Take a card, any card ... Physical exercise and practise make muscles stronger and movements more skilled. In the mind, the same applies to memory. Mental exercise, using your memory and practising how to recall all help you to remember better and faster.

👆 TRY IT YOURSELF

There are ways to improve your memory. These are called memory tricks. For example, use the first letters from the names of the items to make up a weird word. For this picture, it could be ...... This trick may seem difficult at first, but soon gets easier with practice.

INSTANT FACTS

A **newborn baby** probably sleeps for **20 hours** out of every 24.

Most **10-year-old children need about 10 hours** of sleep nightly.

Adults usually need 7–8 hours of sleep each night.

Some people are best with more than eight hours of sleep while others make do with six or less.

If a person is **deprived of a few hours' sleep**, then he or she 'catches up' on most of it over the next couple of sleep sessions.

HEALTHWATCH

Lack of sleep can harm the body faster than lack of food. A person who cannot sleep becomes tired, confused and forgetful, and suffers headaches. He or she may even hear imaginary voices and see imaginary scenes, be unable to talk or listen, and lose touch with the real world.

BRAIN *Wide Awake, Fast Asleep*

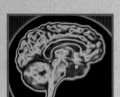

It has been a long and exciting day. You have been wide awake, looking and learning, talking and listening. Yet five minutes after laying down in bed, you are fast asleep. But the brain is far from 'switched off'.

ALERT TO ASLEEP The part of the brain that controls our level of alertness is called the thalamus. Situated in the centre of the whole brain, it looks like two eggs side by side. The thalamus checks information coming in from the senses and the spinal cord, even when we sleep, to see whether it is important or not. If not, then it does not disturb the rest of the brain. But if there is a sudden loud noise, or a jolt, or perhaps a dangerous smell like smoke, the thalamus wakes up the rest of the brain.

UPS & DOWNS OF SLEEP Shortly after we fall asleep, the body becomes very relaxed. Our heartbeat, breathing and digestive system slow down. Most of our muscles become loose and floppy. This state is called deep sleep. About an hour later, our muscles start to twitch. Breathing becomes faster and shallower, and our eyes flick about, even though the eyelids stay closed. This state is called REM (rapid eye movement) sleep. After around 20 minutes, the body relaxes again into deep sleep. These changes from deep to REM sleep happen every hour or two through the night. The deep sleep gradually becomes lighter each time, until eventually we wake up.

OUR IMAGINATION SEEMS TO GO WILD IN DREAMS. *Most people have several dreams each night, during REM sleep. But we usually remember a dream only if we wake up during or just after it. This illustration shows the famous writer Charles Dickens having a vivid dream.*

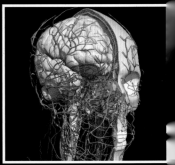

IN FOCUS
NO REST FOR THE BRAIN

Dolphins sleep with only one side of the brain at a time. The other side stays alert, receiving information from the eyes and other senses. If danger approaches the dolphin can react quickly without having to wake up.

Many body parts have a much reduced blood supply during sleep. But the brain requires as much blood as when awake, supplied by the carotid arteries.

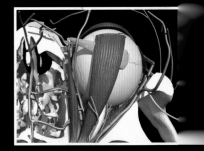

Several sets of muscles become active during REM sleep. Limbs twitch, lips quiver, and of course the six strap-like extra-ocular muscles behind each eyeball produce the eye movements.

WHY DO WE YAWN? No one really knows. It may be to get some fresher air into the lungs after slow, shallow breathing. It may be to exercise the face muscles, which encourages more blood to flow to them and to the brain as well.

THE THALAMUS IS IMPORTANT IN LEVELS OF ALERTNESS OR CONSCIOUSNESS, from very excited and 'buzzing' to deeply asleep. Exactly why we sleep is still not clear. The brain could be sorting out the events of the day, storing important information as memories and getting rid of the rest.

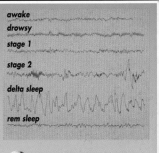

awake
drowsy
stage 1
stage 2
delta sleep
rem sleep

🔧 SLEEP PATTERNS

During sleep the nerve cells of the brain are still active. This is shown by the pattern of the brain's electrical signals while asleep. Shortly after we fall asleep we are very relaxed, but become more anxious during certain periods of sleep.

✋ TRY IT YOURSELF

Some nights we just cannot get to sleep. This is not a problem if it happens now and again. It helps to be not too hot, not too cold, and not too stuffy with some fresh air. If thoughts keep racing through your mind, try to think of peaceful places and happy times like holidays and relaxing in the sun by the sea, with the waves gently lapping on the shore, swish, swish ... zzzzzz.

An eyeball is almost a perfect sphere, measuring 24 mm across and the same from front to back, and 23.5 mm from top to bottom.

People with short sight (myopia) tend to have **bigger eyeballs**, about 28–29 mm.

People with long sight (hypermetropia) usually have **smaller eyeballs**, around 20–21 mm.

👁 HEALTHWATCH

Eyes are so precious that they need great care. Visors, goggles and similar protection shield them against injury and flying particles. These can be darkened when the eyes are at risk from too much light, like bright sunshine, glare off sand or snow, or the intense shine from equipment such as welding torches. A regular visit to the optician is also important. Looking into the eye can detect problems so they can be treated before they become serious.

SENSES *Eyes & Sight*

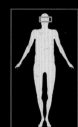

More than half of the knowledge and memories in the brain come in through the eyes, as written words, pictures, diagrams and scenes. Each eye detects light rays and their patterns of brightness, colour and movement, and changes these into patterns of nerve signals for the brain.

PICKING UP LIGHT The eyeball has a white outer covering or sclera. At the front is the coloured iris. It has a hole in the middle called the pupil, where light rays shine into the eye. These rays pass through the clear jelly inside the eyeball and hit the retina. The retina contains more than 120 million microscopic cells called rods and cones. Each of these cells sends nerve signals when light rays hit it. The rods work well in dim light but see only shades of grey, from almost white to almost black. The cones work only in bright light but they see colours and details .

THE IRIS CAN BE BLUE, GREEN, GREY OR BROWN depending on the amount of melanin in the iris. Blue eyes have the least melanin and are more sensitive to light.

🔍 AROUND THE EYE

Arching over the top of the front of the eyeball is the lachrymal gland, which makes tears. Around the sides and rear are six small, ribbon-shaped muscles which swivel the eyeball in its socket. The socket is padded with soft fat for smooth movement.

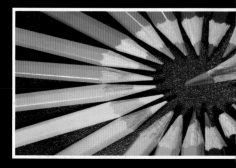

EYELIDS PROTECT THE EYE FROM TOO MUCH LIGHT by automatically squinting. They close instantly if something comes too close to your eye. Every time you blink cleansing tears containing germ fighting chemicals clean your eyes and stop them from drying out.

ALL ANIMALS HAVE TEARS, BUT ONLY HUMANS CRY WHEN THEY ARE UNHAPPY OR HURT. Emotional tears aren't like the ones that are used to clean your eyeball when you blink, they are made up of different chemicals. No one knows why your body produces emotional tears, but when you are sad it can make you feel better to have a good cry.

eye muscles   sclera

iris

The sclera is the tough white coating of the eyeball.

NEAR & FAR How can we judge if objects are near or far away? Each eye moves up, down and side to side by six small, strap-like muscles behind it. Stretch sensors in the muscles signal to the brain about the angle at which the eye looks. If both eyes look at a nearby object, they point inwards slightly. The more they angle inwards, the nearer the object, and the sensors detect this. There are also stretch sensors in the muscle which adjusts the thickness of the lens. The lens becomes thick to focus on nearer objects clearly, and thin for faraway ones. We also compare sizes of objects we know, and how colours and details fade as they get farther away, to judge distance.

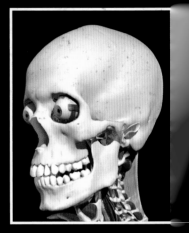

The eyes are almost forward outgrowths of the brain, expanded at the front into ball shapes which detect light. Each nestles well protected by skull bones in the orbit (eye socket).

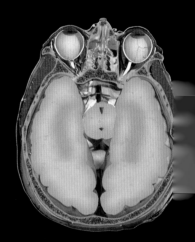

A cutaway across the middle of the head shows the short, stalk-like optic nerve connecting each eye to the brain. This nerve is by far the most complex sensory nerve, containing more than one million message-carrying fibres

THERE ARE THREE DIFFERENT KINDS OF CONE CELLS IN YOUR RETINA. They detect red, blue and green. Light stimulates different combinations of these cones to produce all the different colours you see. In some people one or more of their groups of cones are missing or do not work properly. They may get the colours red and green mixed up or even see things just in black and white and green. This is called colourblindness.

TRY IT YOURSELF

The brain takes cues from images received from the eyes to help it interpret what is being seen. Occasionally these images can trick the brain. Which of the two vertical line segments is longer? Although your visual system tells you that the right one is longer, they are equal in length.

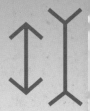

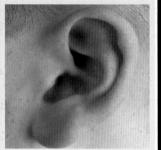

On the scale of pitch (high or low frequency), **ears can detect sounds from 25 to 20,000 vibrations per second**. Dogs can detect much deeper and much higher sounds than this.

On the decibel scale of volume, sounds **over 95 dB can harm our ears**, especially if they go on too long. That includes very loud talking, building work and aircraft noise.

The area of the brain that analyses nerve signals representing sounds is called the auditory cortex.

SENSES *Ears & Hearing*

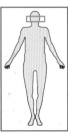

It's amazing how the mind can 'shut out' sounds. As you read these words, concentrating on vision, your ears are hearing noises around you. Yet your brain tends to ignore them – unless there's a sudden strange sound, or you hear your name.

INTO THE EAR HOLE When sound waves hit our ears, they go into the hole in the middle of the ear flap, on the side of the head. Across the end of this tunnel is a flap of skin, the eardrum. It shakes or vibrates as the waves hit. Attached to the eardrum are a chain of three tiny bones called the hammer, anvil and stirrup. (These bones were given their names long ago, when blacksmiths and horses were more common than today!)

SOME SOUNDS ARE TOO LOUD FOR OUR EARS. We put hands over our ears so we do not deafen ourselves!

Ears look tough on the outside, but are very delicate inside. Sometimes germs get into the ear and a sticky fluid, mucus, collects. It causes earache and stops the eardrum or bones from moving freely. Poking things into the ear cannot help, and may be harmful. The problem needs a check by a doctor.

TRY IT YOURSELF

Even if you close your eyes, you can usually hear the direction of a sound from one side – because you have two ears. The sound waves reach the nearer ear about 1/1,300th of a second before the other ear. They are louder in the nearer ear too. The brain detects these differences and works out the sound's direction. But try tilting your head to one side, so your ears point up and down – can you tell a sound's direction then?

THE EAR TUBE OR CANAL HAS A LINING OF HAIRS AND STICKY WAX that traps bits of dust and dirt. As we speak and eat, jaw movements make the old wax loosen and move outwards, cleaning the tube naturally.

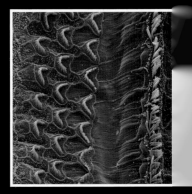

Inside each cochlea are more than 20,000 tiny hair cells, each with 50–100 even tinier hairs. The outer hair cells are arranged in three rows and the hairs on each one form a V or U pattern.

SOUNDS The ear bones vibrate too, and pass their movements to another part, called the cochlea. This is filled with liquid, shaped like a snail and about the size of a sugar cube. Inside, wound around its coil, is an incredibly delicate layer with thousands of microscopic cells that have even smaller hairs. The vibrations pass into the liquid and make these hairs vibrate too, which causes their cells to fire off nerve signals to the brain.

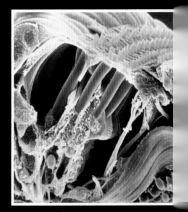

The hair cells (red) have a tall, column-like shape. Their hairs, known as stereocilia (yellow), do not project freely into the fluid in the cochlea. They are loosely embedded in an arch-shaped layer, the tectorial membrane, which vibrates with sound waves.

INNER EAR

The eardrum is about the size of the nail on the little finger – but thinner than this page of paper. It connects via the ear bones (ossicles) to the curly-shaped cochlea, which is only 9 mm across at its base and 5 mm tall.

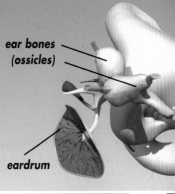

cochlea

ear bones (ossicles)

eardrum

muscles

The gravity sensors in the inner ear can **detect a change of position of less than one degree** (1/360th of a circle).

The nerve carrying balance information to the brain, **the vestibular nerve, has about 19,000 nerve fibres**.

All over the body there are more than **one million stretch sensors** in the muscles, joints, skin and other parts.

SENSES *BALANCING ACT*

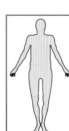

Balance is sometimes called the 'sixth sense'. However, it is not a sense in its own right. It is really a process which goes on all the time, involving various senses and many muscles. Even your eyes help you stay upright!

BALANCE AND THE EAR Every second, the brain receives millions of signals from all over the body, which it uses for the process of balance and staying upright. Many signals come from deep in each ear, near the part involved in hearing, the cochlea. Liquid-filled chambers next to the cochlea have tiny lumps of crystals in them. These hang down by the pull of gravity or swing around with head movements. The lumps pull on nerves which send signals to the brain about the head's position and motion.

JUST AS WE CAN LEARN TO READ OR WRITE, WE CAN LEARN TO BALANCE BETTER. Tiny stretch sensors in muscles and joints allow us to 'feel' the position and posture of body parts. This is known as the proprioceptive sense.

◉ **HEALTHWATCH**

Being whirled around on roller-coaster rides is fun. The movements confuse the sensors inside the ears as the liquid and crystal lumps slosh around. Staying still for a short time afterwards lets the giddiness fade. But some health problems, like Meniere's Disease, cause this giddiness all the time, so you feel as if you are spinning or falling even when lying still.

ABOUT TWO-THIRDS OF ASTRONAUTS BECOME 'SPACESICK'. There is no gravity to pull on the position sensors inside the ears. So there are no clues to being upright or upside down. In fact, in space there is no up or down.

IN FOCUS
BALANCE CELLS

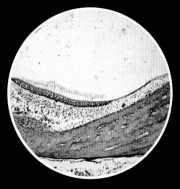

The macula is a patch of hair cells in a fluid-filled chamber next to the cochlea. Their tiny hairs are embedded in a thin layer of jelly-like crystals.

CATS DON'T HAVE NINE LIVES – BUT THEY DO HAVE BETTER BALANCE and can react four times faster than us. They can twist during a fall, arch the back and get the legs ready to take the shock of landing. People learn to fall too, such as parachutists.

SWIRLING AROUND Deep in the ear are a set of three C-shaped tubes – the semicircular canals. Near the end of each tube is another tiny lump, which also pulls on nerve endings as the liquid in the tube swirls around with the head movements. There are also micro-sensors inside muscles and joints all over the body. These tell the brain the positions of joints and whether our muscles are flexed or not. The sensors tell you where your arms, fingers, legs and feet are! Finally, the skin of your feet feels pressure which varies as you lean different ways. This helps with balance too.

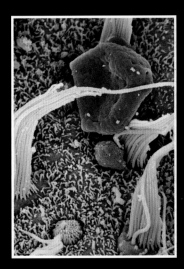

With the crystal layer removed the tiny hairs, stereocilia, can be seen as bundles sticking up from their hair cells. As the head moves, gravity pulls the crystal layer in different directions and bends the hairs, making their cells send nerve signals to the brain

TRY IT YOURSELF

Eyes are important for balance. Stand on one leg with eyes open. It should be fairly easy. Do the same with eyes closed. Without sight, you begin to wobble. Make sure you open your eyes again so you don't fall.

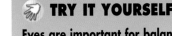

cochlea

semicircular canal

MADE FOR BALANCE

The main balance parts inside the ear are the semicircular canals, and behind them in this view, two chambers called the utricle and saccule. The canals sense head movements while the two chambers detect gravity and the position of the head by their maculae.

Take a good sniff. There are almost certainly smells in the air around you. But maybe your nose and brain have got used to them. This is one of the many extraordinary features of the smelly sense.

SMELL PATCHES The nose's two holes are called the nostrils. They lead into twin air spaces called the nasal chambers. In the top of each chamber is an area of specialised lining about the size of a thumbnail. It is called the olfactory epithelium, or the smell patch. It has an astonishing 25 million tall, thin smell cells, packed together like the pile of a tiny carpet. Each of these smell cells has about 10 even smaller hairs called cilia, sticking down from it into the air space of the nasal chamber below.

HORRIBLE SMELLS WARN US OF ROT AND DECAY AND GERMS. *This tells us not to eat food that has gone bad, or touch items that could make us ill with infection.*

OUR SENSE OF SMELL IS FAIRLY POOR COMPARED TO MANY ANIMALS. *We have about 50 million smell cells, but a dog has 500 million and its sense of smell is probably 1,000 times better than our own.*

Most people can tell apart up to **10,000 different smells**, scents and odours.

One of the most **powerful smells is made by the chemicals called mercaptans**. These are present in skunk spray, and we can detect them at the tiny amounts of one part in 25 billion.

Some nerve signals for smell go to the parts of the brain dealing with emotions and memories, which is why some **smells bring back such strong feelings**.

HEALTHWATCH

Smell is an early warning system. We can smell many dangerous, harmful or poisonous substances. But some deadly fumes have no smell. They include carbon monoxide and carbon dioxide, made by certain forms of burning, such as vehicle engines. This is why vehicle engines should never run in an enclosed space like a garage.

IN FOCUS
SMELL PATCHES AND HAIRS

MOST PEOPLE'S NOSES WORK IN THE SAME WAY. They send the same patterns of nerve signals to the brain. But experts on scents and odours train their minds to concentrate on the details of a smell, which other people miss.

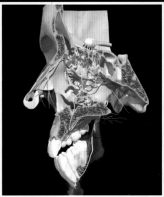

A good sniff makes more air swirl around in the upper nasal chambers, bringing more smell particles to be detected. Just above the smell patches is a bulge, the olfactory bulb (yellow blob), which then extends as the olfactory nerve into the brain.

STICKY LANDINGS Smells are actually tiny particles that drift through the air. They pass through the nasal chamber whenever we breathe in. Some of these particles fit into 'landing sites' on the cilia, in the way that toy shapes like stars and squares fit into the holes of their board. If a smell particle slots into a cilia's landing site, that smell cell sends a nerve signal to the brain.

THE NASAL CHAMBERS INSIDE THE NOSE ARE TALL AIR SPACES WITH SHELF-LIKE RIDGES of bone (conchae) sticking out from the sides. There is a smell patch in the top or roof of each chamber.

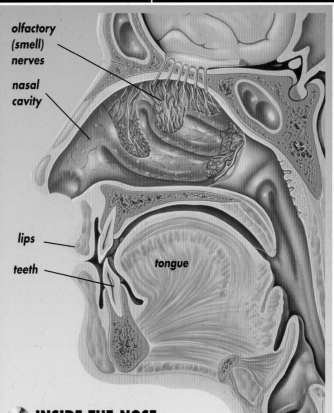

olfactory (smell) nerves

nasal cavity

lips

teeth

tongue

🔧 INSIDE THE NOSE

The smell patches are in the upper part of each nasal chamber. Tiny nerve branches gather signals from them and join to the olfactory bulb above. This 'pre-sorts' the nerve signals before they pass into the brain.

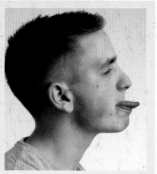

A young person has a total of about **10,000 taste buds**.

This number falls by middle age to about 8,000, and **in old age to nearer 5,000**.

This is partly **why older people say that 'foods today have less taste** than when I was young'.

Some people have fewer than 1,000 taste buds while others possess more than 20,000.

👁 HEALTHWATCH

Ouch! It hurts when you bite your tongue or lip. This usually happens because you are thinking of something else, rather than eating. Or perhaps you are trying to talk and chew at the same time. Such damaged areas usually heal in a day or two. However, they may turn into raw, red areas called ulcers, which hurt and sting when you eat. The doctor or pharmacist can advise on treatment.

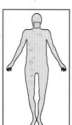

Your tongue is very useful, and not only for tasting food and drink. It can moisten your lips and lick bits of food from them, move food around in your mouth as you chew, change its shape and position as you speak clearly, and even make an appearance outside the mouth which is a sign of rudeness.

PIMPLES & BUDS The tongue is made up almost entirely of muscle. It has a thin covering that protects this muscle, covered with small pimple-like bumps and flaps called papillae. These are especially large and lumpy across the back of the tongue. On and around each of these are much smaller sensors called taste buds, each one too small to see. There are many thousands of taste buds at the front, sides and rear of the tongue, but very few in the main middle area.

TONGUES HAVE MANY JOBS, especially keeping the lips, teeth and gums clean. Also, try talking without moving your tongue!

LIKE SMELL, TASTE IS AN EARLY WARNING SYSTEM for items we might eat and swallow. Some sour and bitter tastes warn us that foods may be rotten or mouldy, and could cause food poisoning.

OUT IN THE WILD, animals trust their instincts and avoid bad-tasting foods. Tongues are also useful for licking skin and fur clean.

THE SIGHT AND SMELL OF FOOD CAUSES A BODILY REACTION, where watery saliva (spit) flows into the mouth. This saliva moistens the food so it is easier to chew. It also releases flavour particles from the food so it is easier to taste.

IN FOCUS
TASTE BUDS

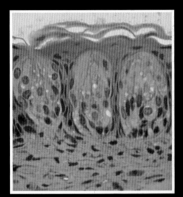

The taste buds are positioned mainly on the sides of the papillae and around their bases, rather than on the flat tongue surface.

FLAVOURS GALORE? Our taste buds look a bit like tiny oranges. Each taste bud has taste cells that look like the segments of the fruit. Each taste cell has tiny hairs called cilia at its tip, just like the smell cells found in the nose. Food and drink has different flavours because of different taste particles. Each flavour has a different shape, and if it fits into a 'landing site' on the cilia, then the taste cells send nerve signals to the brain. The vast number of flavours we appreciate are produced by the combination of these tastes with smell. This is why we can't appreciate food properly when we have a cold.

TASTE ZONES

We sense different basic flavours on different parts of the tongue. Sweet flavours are detected mainly at the front tip, salty ones along the front sides, sour along the rear sides, and bitter across the back.

TONGUE

bitter

sour   sour

salty   salty

sweet

THE CHAMELEON LIZARD'S TONGUE IS ALMOST AS LONG AS ITS WHOLE BODY! If your tongue was this length, you could flick it out to grab food which was too far away for your hands to reach.

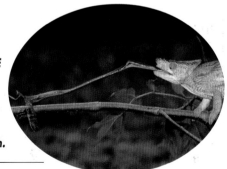

TRY IT YOURSELF

With the dampened end of a drinking straw, put a few sugar grains on the tip of your tongue. Let them dissolve and taste the sweetness. Wash your mouth out and do the same, but put the grains towards the middle rear of your tongue. Can you taste anything?

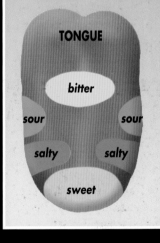

In the sensitive skin of the fingertips there are **50–100 micro-sensors in an area the size of this o.**

In the much less sensitive skin on the small of the back or **outside of the thigh, the same area has just 1–5 microsensors**.

We can **detect temperature differences of only 1–2°C.** For most people about 42–43°C is comfortably warm, while 46–47°C is uncomfortably hot.

◉ HEALTHWATCH

Pain may be a pain, but it is also useful. It warns the brain that part of the body is about to suffer damage, or has already been injured. This allows us to avoid the harm, or care for the injured part. Ignoring pain, or taking too many pills without medical advice to relieve it, could make the damage worse.

SENSES *Skin & Touch*

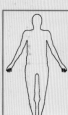

What can you feel right now? You might be touching the pages of this book, but what else? Your clothes and footwear, although perhaps you had forgotten about them. Perhaps you are touching a table or chair too. The body is always in contact with something.

SKIN SENSATIONS Whenever our skin is pressed, microscopic touch sensors just under its surface are stretched and squashed. When this happens, the sensors fire off nerve signals along very thin nerve fibres. The fibres gather together to form thicker nerves which carry the signals from all over the body to the brain. We also feel 'touch' even when something brushes against the hairs yet does not contact the skin. This is because these hairs have nerve endings wrapped around them. These also send signals to the brain as the hairs are moved.

PETS FEEL WARM AND SOFT, which are both pleasing sensations of touch. Stroking them helps us to relax.

The lips are one of the most sensitive parts of the body because they have lots of touch sensors packed together in a small space. This is one of the reasons why babies and young children often put things to their mouths to investigate them - and why adults enjoy kissing!

IN FOCUS
PACINIAN SENSORS

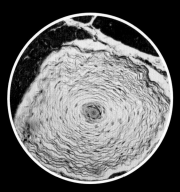

Pressure on the skin is detected by pacinian sensors. These are buried in the deeper skin layer and shaped like tiny squashed onions. They may be more than one millimetre long.

WHY IS TICKLING FUNNY? No one knows. But it works best if the tickler uses a light touch, with a regular brushing motion, and moves gradually across the skin. Surprise is also important – it's very difficult to tickle yourself!

MANY KINDS OF TOUCH FEELINGS Like all of our senses, touch is more complicated than it seems. There are different sizes and shapes of microsensors in the skin, and they respond in different ways, sending complex patterns of nerve signals to the brain. These patterns let us know the type of touch we are receiving. The signals also tell us if the item we are touching is warm or cold, smooth or rough, hard or soft, and still or moving.

WE CAN LEARN COMPLEX MOVEMENTS BY TOUCH ALONE, without having to look, from tying shoelaces to playing music. The brain concentrates on the feelings from the hands and fingers, and moves the muscles in well-practised ways.

TRY IT YOURSELF

We can identify an object and build up a picture of it in the brain, just by touch. Place about eight common items on a table, close your eyes, and pick up one. You probably know what it is straight away by its size, shape and feel, from hard, cool metal to softer wood, smooth plastic or squishy sponginess.

SKIN SENSORS

There are about eight different kinds of microscopic sensors in the skin. The largest are about half a millimetre across, the smallest 100 times tinier.

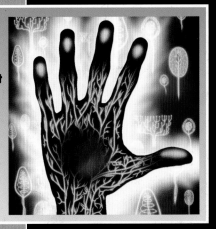

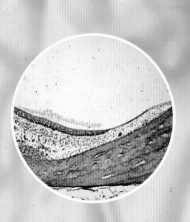

AUDITORY To do with the sense of hearing, for example, the auditory nerve carries nerve signals from the cochlea deep in the ear, to the brain.

AUTONOMIC NERVOUS SYSTEM Parts of the nerve system which deal with 'automatic' body processes, that we do not have to think about controlling, such as heartbeat and digesting food.

AXON The long, wire-like part extending from a nerve cells, also called a nerve fibre, which passes nerve signals onwards to other cell.

BRAIN STEM The lower, narrower part at the base of the brain, which extends downwards and tapers into the spinal cord. It deals mainly with automatic body processes like the heartbeat.

CELLS Tiny parts or building-blocks of the body, which in their billions form larger parts like bones, muscles and skin.

CENTRAL NERVOUS SYSTEM The brain and spinal cord.

CEREBELLUM The small, lower rear part of the brain, with a wrinkled surface, which is mainly involved in controlling movements.

CEREBROSPINAL FLUID A liquid found between the innermost (pia mater) and middle (arachnoid) layers of the meninges, around the brain and spinal cord. It helps to cushion and protect the brain.

CEREBRUM The large, upper, domed, wrinkled part of the brain, consisting of two halves, the cerebral hemispheres.

CILIA Tiny hair-like projections of microscopic cells, found in many body parts. Cilia on the smell and taste cells respond to certain chemical substances carrying odours or flavours.

COCHLEA The small, curly, snail-shaped part deep in the ear, which changes sound vibrations into nerve signals.

CONES Tapering cells in the retina of the eye that sense light rays and colours but work only in bright conditions.

CORTEX The thin, greyish covering of the cerebrum (cerebral hemispheres) – the main part where conscious thinking, awareness, experience of senses and control of muscles occur.

CRANIUM The domed upper part of the skull which covers the brain.

DENDRITES Small, spidery-looking, branched parts extending from the main part or body of a nerve cell, which receive nerve signals from other nerve cells.

DERMIS The inner or lower layer of skin, under the epidermis, which contains blood vessels, hair roots and touch sensors.

EEG Electro-encephalogram, a paper tracing or screen display of wavy, spiky lines that represent nerve signals in the brain, detected by sensor pads stuck to the skin of the head and scalp.

EPIDERMIS The outermost or surface layer of skin, which is mostly dead and continually being worn away.

MENINGES Three very thin layers that wrap closely around the brain and spinal cord, and with the cerebrospinal fluid, cushion them from knocks and jolts.

MOTOR In the body, to do with muscles and movements, for example, a motor nerve carries nerve signals from the brain out to muscles to control their movements.

NERVE A long, cord-like body part that carries information in the form of tiny pulses of electricity called nerve signals.

NEURON A nerve cell specially designed in shape to receive and pass on nerve signals.

OLFACTORY To do with the sense of smell, for example, the olfactory

epithelium is the 'smell patch' inside the nose where odours are detected.

PAPILLAE On the tongue, the small but visible lumps and 'pimples' that give it a rough surface and house the much smaller tastes buds.

PERIPHERAL NERVOUS SYSTEM The system of nerves that branch from the brain and spinal cord.

RETINA The very thin inner lining of the eyeball, which changes patterns of light rays into nerve signals.

RODS Tall, rounded cells in the retina of the eye, which sense light rays and work in dim conditions but do not detect colours.

SPINAL CORD The main nerve extending from the base of the brain, along the inside the backbone (spinal column).

SPINAL NERVES Nerves that branch off the spinal cord, between the individual bones or vertebrae of the backbone (spinal column).

TASTE BUD A tiny cluster of cells, far too small to seen, that detects tastes.

VERTEBRAE The individual bones which make up the body's backbone or spinal column.

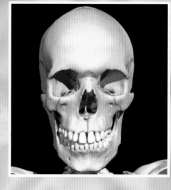

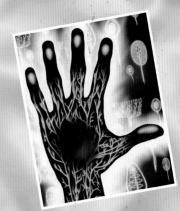
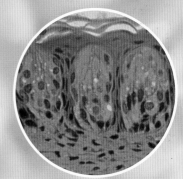

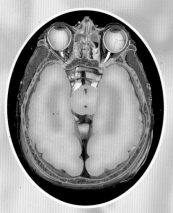

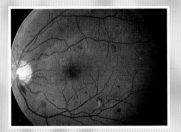

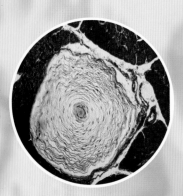

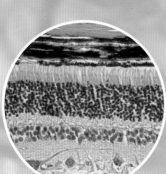

Copyright © ticktock Entertainment Ltd 2004
First published in Great Britain in 2004 by ticktock Media Ltd.,
Unit 2, Orchard Business Centre, North Farm Road, Tunbridge Wells, Kent, TN2 3XF
We would like to thank: Elizabeth Wiggans and Jenni Rainford for their help with this book.
ISBN 1 86007 561 4 HB   ISBN 1 86007 557 6 PB
Printed in China
A CIP catalogue record for this book is available from the British Library.

Picture Credits
Alamy: OFCl. 5r, 12tl, 15bc, 16-17, 19tc, 21tc, 22-23c, 24-25c. Mediscan: 27tr. Primal Pictures: OFCr, 7t, 11r, 13tr, 17tr, 17cr, 19tr, 19cr, 25tr.
Science Photo Library: 7c, 7br, 10-11c, 11cr, 13br, 15tr, 15cr, 21tr, 21cr, 23cr, 25br. 29br, 29tr.